# CLIMBING

# BACK

# THE NATIONAL POETRY SERIES

The National Poetry Series was established in 1978 to ensure the publication of five poetry books annually through participating publishers. Publication is funded by the Copernicus Society of America, the Lannan Foundation, and the National Endowment for the Arts.

*1999 Competition Winners*

Tenaya Darlington of Wisconsin, *Madame Deluxe*
Chosen by Lawson Inada, to be published by Coffee House Press

Eugene Gloria of Massachusetts, *Drivers at the Short-Time Motel*
Chosen by Yusef Komunyakaa, to be published by Viking Penguin

Corey Marks of Texas, *Renunciation*
Chosen by Philip Levine, to be published by University of Illinois Press

Dionisio D. Martínez of Florida, *Climbing Back*
Chosen by Jorie Graham, to be published by W. W. Norton & Company

Standard Schaefer of California, *Nova*
Chosen by Nick Piombino, to be published by Sun & Moon Press

# CLIMBING

# BACK

POEMS

Dionisio D. Martínez

W. W. Norton & Company

New York • London

For information about permission to reprint selections from this book, write to
Permissions, W. W. Norton & Company, Inc., 500 Fifth Avenue, New York, NY 10110

The text of this book is composed in Adobe Garamond with the display set in Castellar
Composition by Julia Druskin
Manufacturing by Courier Companies, Inc.
Book design by Chris Welch

Library of Congress Cataloging-in-Publication Data
Martínez, Dionisio D., 1956–
Climbing back /  by Dionisio D. Martínez
p.  cm.
**ISBN 0-393-05006-8**
I. Title.

PS3563.A733334 C58 2000
811'.54—dc21                                    00-040211

W. W. Norton & Company, Inc., 500 Fifth Avenue, New York, N.Y. 10110
www.wwnorton.com

W. W. Norton & Company Ltd., 10 Coptic Street, London WC1A  1PU

1  2  3  4  5  6  7  8  9  0

*For Warren Hampton*

# ACKNOWLEDGMENTS

I'd like to thank the editors of the publications in which these poems first appeared:

*The American Poetry Review:* "The Prodigal Son and the two Sinatras," "The Prodigal Son on Green Dolphin Street," "The Prodigal Son learns the word 'antebellum,'" "The Prodigal Son, briefly suspected in the shooting of Andy Warhol, is cleared of all charges," "The Prodigal Son: Temporary trains," "The Prodigal Son in his own words: Debussy"

*Blue Mesa Review:* "The Prodigal Son investigates the Hemingway suicides," "The Prodigal Son in his own words: Homage to Li Po," "The Prodigal Son, for whom summer is a verb"

*The Carolina Quarterly:* "The Prodigal Son: Standard deviations"

*Chattahoochee Review:* "The Prodigal Son swims to a barrier island," "The Prodigal Son in Pompeii," "The Prodigal Son envisions nothing"

*Colorado Review:* "The Prodigal Son as understudy," "The Prodigal Son locates the epicenter," "The Prodigal Son: Notes from the epicenter," "The Prodigal Son in absentia"

*Confrontation:* "The Prodigal Son: Kierkegaard at face value,"

"The Prodigal Son reassesses Kierkegaard," "The Prodigal Son forgives his brother," "The Prodigal Son on a bus in New Delhi"

*Connecticut Review:* "The Prodigal Son is caught off guard by planned obsolescence," "The Prodigal Son in a frenzy of scarves"

*Denver Quarterly:* "The Prodigal Son edits a newsreel," "The Prodigal Son deconstructs the origami language," "The Prodigal Son overhears his interrogators"

*The Eckerd College Review:* "The Prodigal Son in his own words: Letter to the anarchists," "The Prodigal Son takes up a hobby," "The Prodigal Son: Studies for a portrait of John Merrick"

*The Georgia Review:* "The Prodigal Son paraphrases a plagiarist"

*Green Mountains Review:* "The Prodigal Son as decoy," "The Prodigal Son in his own words: Captivity"

*Harvard Review:* "The Prodigal Son accidentally kneels while learning to crawl"

*Indiana Review:* "The Prodigal Son in his own words: Bees"

*The Iowa Review:* "The Prodigal Son, Mr. DeMille, Norma Desmond, Billy Wilder, Claude Monet, et al."

*The Journal:* "The Prodigal Son's education," "The Prodigal Son stands outside the Dakota"

*The Kenyon Review:* "The Prodigal Son in his own words: Credo"

*Luna:* "The Prodigal Son in his own words: Free will," "The Prodigal Son in spite of himself"

*The Marlboro Review:* "The Prodigal Son: The treadmill effect"

*The Massachusetts Review:* "The Prodigal Son loses his wife," "The Prodigal Son buys a new car"

*Mid-American Review:* "The Prodigal Son in his own words: Benedictus," "The Prodigal Son watches a documentary," "The Prodigal Son gives blood"

*The New Republic:* "The Prodigal Son, accompanied by the

ideogram," "The Prodigal Son paces the other half of a semicircle," "The Prodigal Son in his own words: Fate"

*North American Review:* "The Prodigal Son considers a diplomatic career," "The Prodigal Son: Vegas, after hours," "The Prodigal Son and the epistemology of chance"

*Prairie Schooner:* "The Prodigal Son marks his calendar," "The Prodigal Son in his own words: Independence"

*The Prose Poem: An International Journal:* "The Prodigal Son: Amnesty," "The Prodigal Son is spotted on the grassy knoll"

*Quarterly West:* "The Prodigal Son: Still life in slow motion," "The Prodigal Son learns to drown"

*Sarasota Review of Poetry:* "The Prodigal Son in his own words: Faith," "The Prodigal Son succumbs to secular miracles"

*Seneca Review:* "The Prodigal Son pulls an all-nighter," "The Prodigal Son in his own words: Rhetorical answers," "The Prodigal Son confronting Zeno's paradoxes," "The Prodigal Son in his own words: Tipping over the actuarial tables"

*Solo:* "The Prodigal Son in his own words: Prayer against Ecclesiastes," "The Prodigal Son bribes the fortune teller"

*Tampa Review:* "The Prodigal Son buries a dog named Pavlov"

*Verse:* "The Prodigal Son: Science fiction," "The Prodigal Son jumps bail," "The Prodigal Son introduces George W. G. Ferris," "The Prodigal Son: German postcards," "The Prodigal Son catches up with the bounty hunters"

"The Prodigal Son loses his wife" and "The Prodigal Son buys a new car" were reprinted in *El Coro* (Martín Espada, ed.; University of Massachusetts Press, 1997); "The Prodigal Son and the two Sinatras" and "The Prodigal Son: Still life in slow motion" were reprinted in *La Pérdida y el Suenho* (Carlos Espinosa, ed.; Centro Cultural Espanhol, 2000).

I am deeply indebted to Kathleen Wakefield, whose keen observations gave the manuscript a path to follow long before it was assembled.

While these pages were in limbo, I was kept afloat by the support and encouragement of Cecilia Denegri, Stephen Dunn, Judith Kitchen, Dick & Caren Lobo, Ana Menéndez, Mary Elizabeth Pérez, Kathryn VanSpanckeren, and my mother, Manuela Méndez.

Many thanks to the National Endowment for the Arts and to the John Simon Guggenheim Memorial Foundation for fellowships that enabled me to complete this collection; to all involved in the National Poetry Series and in the foundations that support it; to Ryan Meany; to Drake Bennett; and to my editor, Jill Bialosky.

Jorie Graham, I am grateful beyond words.

# CONTENTS

# 2

## CODA

# PREFACE

This is a book of contingency plans. Also a book of interstellar (and intercultural) nightmares, a crashed party called civilization. As it says about our appetite for traffic: we have been written and we've been erased, but we sprout again from cracks in the road. It suggests you try deciphering that foreign tongue in your mouth. It suggests you have been mightily distracted and might want to try to find (under conditions that are impossible, of course, or "only possible elsewhere") your way home. Where time goes when it's not in a hurry. Where thought revisits itself. Where you are the stranger you pass on the street, your own second chance. Forget gravity, being *here* is the only chance you have, selfhood the beginning of something insistently circular: go home. It's all a shortcut—immortality, chance, improvisation, faith; it's all uphill (Satchmo dropping his lyrics midsong) (story striking back like a snake) (rain and words scatting off each other); it's all souvenir, this tale of dazed survivals told by a child with absolute pitch, wearing a body inside out, turning the heart into a public spectacle. Heartbreaking, overstuffed, seeping with history, lonelier than imaginable and truly in-the-face of American culture, *Climbing Back*'s debris-field of prose poems tries with all its heart to outrun cultural paradigms and ends up refining our spiritual ignorance till it's our most gorgeous attribute.

—Jorie Graham

MARCUS AURELIUS: You have perhaps seen a severed hand or foot, or a head lying by itself apart from its body. That is the state to which a man is doing his best to reduce himself, when he refuses to accept what befalls him and breaks away from his fellows, or when he acts for selfish ends alone. Then you become an outcast from the unity of Nature; though born a part of it, you have cut yourself away with your own hand. Yet here is the beautiful thought: that it still lies in your own power to reunite yourself.

COUNT BASIE: Let's try it one more once.

# INTRO

## The Prodigal Son jumps bail

After hovering, after spying like an insect on the screen door, he asks if perhaps there's a place for him at the table. He knows the answer, but likes to hear them say it. Their lungs and then their chests and finally their mouths fill with all the things they'd like to tell him. There was a war, they admit, although that's not what they want to say. There was famine. The house fell and was rebuilt at least three times, always on a different site. Tap water is potable for the first time in years. In the wake of the latest scandal, they tell him, the new government has maintained its innocence, blaming the Constitution, blaming the scholars and "their gross misinterpretation of our laws." They bring him up to date on all the deaths in the family, the marriages, the births. Someone starts to talk about alleged disappearances, but is soon interrupted and the subject is closed. There is only one answer and even the bread crumbs stand at attention when it comes.

1

## The Prodigal Son and the two Sinatras

The first time he becomes aware of the voice, some are saying that popular music is at its nadir. Transition tends to have this effect on people. Nelson Riddle is no longer writing the arrangements. If there's a new audience, it can't sort through the complexities of a big band, the lush trombones, the way a soloist can play his way out of the chart without ever leaving it. The early voice, crooning with the Dorsey outfit, comes to his attention much later. This voice *is* the trombone, the solo that comes face to face with the night and comes out unscathed. Like Monk's hands on the keyboard, it stops in places where one would expect it to become a victim of its own inventions. But it wanders back nonchalantly and you forget the pauses that make it possible. He doesn't know how to reconcile the two voices before they run into each other, both of them losing their timing on the way, both of them trying to catch up with the present. They can't conceive of irretrievable losses, of hearts so still that they're no longer susceptible to music. One voice doesn't hear the other struggling like a cloud on a clear day. Neither one suspects that they will meet here, and these are not compassionate times.

# The Prodigal Son on Green Dolphin Street

or, more precisely, on a distant variation of it. Some things you can never apply to a life at the window, not even at one of the windows where Eliot, in his proper voice, places men in shirtsleeves, tells them to lean out, to shout something at the reader. A rudeness so mannered you know it isn't theirs but Eliot's—or Eliot's idea of rudeness in the common man—and it's Eliot's insults they shout, and Eliot's lips where they place their cigarettes and light them. Let's say it's 1958. Sounds like Miles Davis nearby—a trumpet that knows its limitations and doesn't give a damn. Jazz crosses a line at one point. On this side is the musician, his lips, his lungs. Across the line is the song, the horn, no trace of the man. Say Eliot lives down the street, or is visiting someone down the street, and hears enough to make him stay longer, to make him walk out alone. Sometimes, rereading Eliot, these men are present. Sometimes they're nowhere in the vicinity—it's all empty streets and empty windows, it's as if he meant for the men to peer from the windows only occasionally. Follow this shattered logic for a moment: Miles and Eliot run into each other on one of these streets. Maybe it's an alley, but this is not important. They brush against each other. One of them mutters something, the other looks away. This is *very* important. Eliot has everything by which he'll be remembered behind him and seven years ahead of him. Miles has just played the Plaza Hotel. One of the two men—hard to say which one—is doomed and the street will get the better of him.

# The Prodigal Son: The treadmill effect

is not limited to walking uphill during a landslide. A man can
scat. A man can believe the simple story of Satchmo dropping his
lyrics in midsong. The story can strike back like a snake, biting the
man on the neck. A man can scat until the sounds make sense again,
until the words come back to the page he sets under the one small
leak. It rains and the words talk to each other in a peculiarly inti-
mate language. A man can listen even if he doesn't understand. A
man can go on listening even as he declares war on what he hears.
He can scat successfully only if he doesn't know it is the art of com-
ing undone. Crumbs of sound snap off until the air is empty. A man
can scat for help when the journey is longer than the road. A man
who believes in Satchmo watches him drop his horn and his lyrics
as though this were also the art of falling. Not falling apart or falling
out but simply falling. A man can believe that from an accident an
industry rises. Scat acquires properties one would expect to find in
the synthetic counterpart of speech. A man learning to scat is not
unlike a fire learning to burn. The man picks up the lyric sheet and
the horn. Satchmo walks away like a landslide. The man improvis-
es a story.

# The Prodigal Son: German postcards

## I. ELLA AT DEUTSCHLANDHALLE, WEST BERLIN, 13 FEBRUARY 1960

This is how you wing it when identical souvenirs are exchanged. His hands and the object in his hands immediately turn a single color and texture while her hands refuse to be transformed (though solid, the object conforms to the cupping of her palms, to the fingers following the curve that begins at the center of each palm; a childish instinct records every gesture, leaving out the implicit dangers, so the thought that a corner of the world is safe is more convincing tonight; the object proposes a compromise, the hands decline or dismiss the proposition; she watches the whole affair as if the hands were not hers, as if the hands were empty, as if, as though, as opposed to; she brings her hands together, interlocking fingers falling into place like some military formation, and the object becomes the gap we assume exists between any two things that are joined, no matter how close the union) or the transformation is too slow to be relevant. You be the judge. You in your wing chair. You in your slippers. You reading in your sleep.

## 2. Brandenburg a cappella, 9 November 1989

Sometimes a great architect works undercover in the wrecking crew. He chisels for the enemy. Wall to rubble, rubble to dust. His sweat is genuine, almost biblical. Mercenaries who've joined the project fall until there's no one left up there, nothing to fall from, only fallen men covered with a film as taut as a good alibi. They rise and join the night like coal miners who accidentally save themselves and stumble into their own parade. Even when they grow comfortable with the floats and streamers and the band marching silently behind them, the miners are still surprised to see the wives and children of the victims waving from the sidewalk as if these dazed survivors carried in their dust the essence of the dead.

## The Prodigal Son: Kierkegaard at face value

The child with absolute pitch forgets Mozart, and music stops seeping out of that room where the fire escape skips a few rungs. The silent child wants to panic but can't find the appropriate expression. The crowd appears to grow sensible in the confusion though nothing actually *grows*; no visible sign of sensibility—say, a third eyebrow—makes a spontaneous appearance in the crowd to assure us that it's finally tame. This brings us to the body, the single unanimous body wearing itself inside out. One wonders what pulls it all together, how this and this compensate for a lack of that; why no single part is a threat—to the whole or to the other parts; why there is no sign of a system or hierarchy. The one he follows home stops to ask for directions, consequently turning into a public spectacle. A crowd installs itself to watch or to be seen.

# The Prodigal Son reassesses Kierkegaard

*El odio como factor de lucha . . .*

I.

Jimi Hendrix is playing "Little Wing" and it isn't raining yet. The house shifts a bit every season, the earth below it settling like someone old enough to refer to the town of his adult life as home. The towns of childhood are warmer and vague, and the aunt who smells like soup comes to visit every summer and stays too long. This is the bird that flies into his cupped hands when he stands on the green balcony, his aunt leaning on the piano, watching him and watching the bird fly off and back again. Little wing split in two. Clouds building. One loud dream always tugging at his plaid shirt.

*. . . el odio intransigente al enemigo que impulsa más allá de las limi-taciones naturales del ser humano . . .*

2.

Let's get one thing straight. The wall keeps coming back. His father takes him to the harbor to see the famous ship that keeps its eye on the island, but he sees only sea and sky. His father points, but still he sees no ship. When they come home, the wall he has crushed like paper in so many dreams is back. Though he tries, he cannot see the famous ship, and it becomes a symbol—like God and the enemy. The wall, which few notice, becomes for him what the ship has become for nearly everyone else. He hears of other walls with some evil purpose, but he can only see this one as it turns to paper in his dreams and back to brick in this life.

*. . . y lo convierte en una efectiva, selectiva y fría máquina de matar.*
*Nuestros soldados tienen que ser así, un pueblo sin odio no puede*
*triunfar sobre un enemigo brutal.* —Che Guevara

## 3.

More about the bird though not everything. He has vowed never to tell us all he remembers. He says only one town is approachable enough. The bird, he says. The green balcony overlooking the abandoned gas pump and, beyond that, the furniture store with a single wicker sofa (not for sale) in the showroom. One day, from the balcony, he watches the parade. It features an enemy plane shot down by the rebels. He notices that it has only one wing. By now he knows not to trust the rebels. This makes him the enemy. The bird flies down to the gas pump and its eyes meet the eyes of ordinary humans slowly becoming a crowd.

## The Prodigal Son edits a newsreel

for consistency and the result is enough to make a revisionist weep. It is always difficult to pin down the source of tears, the raw and moist emotion that manifests itself in the eyes. Maybe it starts outside the body and seeps in surreptitiously, swings like a pendulum in the throat. There is a wealth of possibilities on the cutting room floor—buildings to be demolished, voices to obstruct, faces to rearrange in a crowd, faces to pull out of a crowd, fields to be filled with faces, faces to fill with bewilderment. The living know instinctively how to strike a pose; everyone else has to scramble for the items needed to come up with the blueprint and a rudimentary knowledge of the language it speaks. Before the beginning, one has a scene in mind—a brook, a mote, the impression of a body on the tender surface of a recently plowed field. Some revisionists cry because they see the future and it is self-explanatory.

## The Prodigal Son watches a documentary

on euphoria and feels his body—muscle by muscle, limb by limb—fall asleep during the screening. There is an insurrection, there are lynchings, there is a highly combustible gathering of names followed by more lynchings. The time is most likely the present though the place doesn't appear to be particularly attached—in the sense place is sometimes *emotionally* attached (one wishes there were a more reliable term)—to anything historically or geographically measurable. Now and then, one feels on the scene the grip of something not quite scripted. Someone comes by to light the lamps along one street and then another. It is not unlike watching an automobile being pulled by a team of horses. But the glow from the street lamps is consistent with the mood of the mob: violence needs back lighting, like the face of Greta Garbo. (That contrived halo, one suspects, is a compromise hammered out from a clause of unreasonable demands in her contract.) Whether it's Garbo or a mob, the desired effect is always a glimpse of the text one expects to read in the Great Unwritten Contract. Collect enough glimpses and you have a partial image, which is the source of illusion, disillusion, the stop-action sequence of a mythological animal sprouting horns in a fraction of the time it takes you to look up its name.

## The Prodigal Son, Mr. DeMille, Norma Desmond, Billy Wilder, Claude Monet, et al.

He runs into Billy Wilder, the director, at the Paramount lot, and they start to chat about the state of American cinema and how life on the big screen has grown dangerously accustomed to itself. It's like putting on weight over the years, one says, and not noticing what a burden the body has become. Both men are intrigued by the notion of coming back from the dead to recount one's ordinary life. They assume that there are captive ears for this out there, anonymous listeners with equally ordinary lives. The relevance of any one thing is relative. Only relativity is *always* relevant. Both men have an ear to the ground, as they say even now that the expression has lost its luster. The ground will do although other surfaces are safer and more reliable. What they need is a hook, another expression that now and again finds its way to the surface of our vocabulary. Billy suggests a shot from the bottom of the pool, looking up. On the surface, like one of these dormant expressions of our vernacular, a body floats. Beyond it, the usual characters one would expect at the scene of any suspicious death. They appear a bit more distorted than the floating body, and the mansion in the background is as hazy as those Houses of Parliament Monet painted over and over. In some variations, fog dominates the composition. This should not be an impediment. The key to understanding the paintings is to know that they are all *about* buildings, that the presence of buildings is not particularly crucial.

## The Prodigal Son paraphrases a plagiarist

hoping to produce an echo in a vacuum, a rendering versus a carbon of the original. Salvador Dalí has a theory about the *Angelus* of Millet—he is not obsessed with the painting we know but with what he believes Millet paints and eventually paints over. When the Louvre finally X-rays the *Angelus*, revealing something like a child's coffin beneath what is now a basket on the ground between a man and a woman, Dalí says this confirms his premonition and explains why the expressions on the couple's faces bear no relation to the exhaustion of field work. These peasants are not bowing their heads to examine the workmanship of the basket or the ripeness of the fruits it contains; they stand in a room beyond grief, the door locked, grief thrashing about in the hall. Because there are too many keys and most of them are mislabeled, one tends to spend too much time in the dark hall, fighting grief for the right key. There is no mention of the original shape or purpose of the wheelbarrow behind the woman (although one would think this is an elementary problem: every coffin needs a carriage); there are no questions about the pitchfork planted near the man, how it may be a shovel in disguise. Dalí finds the key and makes his way into the room a bit too soon, casually greeting the peasants who are stunned by his appearance. While the unlikely trio denounces surrealism, one could conceivably X-ray every painting in the Louvre and become self-appointed curator of the results; one could create or attract a subculture of those who believe that the only possible art is the discovery of the thing effaced—a voice quivering beneath a still life, a nude killed by a cubist, the Millet child spending the better part of eternity upstaged by uncounted bodies in a mass grave.

## The Prodigal Son gives blood

What could be more intimate? Battlefield, altar, *bodas de sangre,* marriage bed. If it pleases the gods, there's bound to be a con man with a shortcut nearby. The ghost of Hamlet's father is more convincing than the Prince of Denmark in the flesh. Antimatter is more theatrically inclined than matter, just as radio—despite all the arguments for the intimacy of the page or the screen's objectivity—is the medium best equipped to handle suspense. The con man keeps falling between stations, the shortwave set always on the blink, countries fading out, countries fading in, a multitude of unrelated monologues forced to share a single mouth, the listener—this means *you,* Mr. Con Man—never knowing where any station will turn up. (Never twice on the same spot.) "This is Radio Luxembourg." "No, *this* . . ." And the second voice flaunts its anonymity like an echo that returns at will. If this were television and the shadow-voice an image, they would call it a ghost. A clot of massacres jams radio signals. Radio Free Europe, Radio Martí, the pirate voices from offshore—all jammed. A bloodless death is like a downtown flasher who sends his raincoat to the cleaners, waits, goes back to ask why the holdup, is told the raincoat is in someone else's hands, an *honest* mistake. A bloodless coup at the palace and the new leader emerges with a clean raincoat too big at the shoulders. When he waves to his sympathizers (one sees only the man but assumes he isn't waving to an empty street), his own bony shoulders wriggle inside the padded shoulders of the raincoat, they go limp like mice halfway down the length of a snake. A meal as bloody and as bloodless as a ghost. The little man, shoulders like foreign hearts pumping the cold blood of a reptile, has come to hear from a ghost what the radio will not (cannot?) tell him; stops halfway down the steps that lead to the palace gate; takes off his raincoat to beat the air, creating an illusion of wind no ghost can resist.

## The Prodigal Son in a frenzy of scarves

and empty hands above the clearing where the long-distance runner becomes less visible, less symbolic and more efficient. These races—and the glory, should he win—endorse a once subtle self-indulgence. Though not every culmination builds to a false start, he finds it safer to think in those terms. Amnesia has a rich, misunderstood history. He records half-truths in the Rosetta stone of his days until it's gullible enough to swallow the heavy breeze that blows in from the straits, and smooth as silence. The less aromatic trees within earshot blush when he says *rosewood*. If he calls for rose water, every cypress in the marsh kneels like a bride. He gathers—without a clue of the difference between organisms that harbor a single death and those that carry a generous supply—raw materials for a perennial bouquet, calling out their names as he spots them: *rose of Sharon, rose geranium, rosemary, rose of Jericho, rose moss*. The residue in his hands is mostly rose quartz, plain dust or deliverance.

## The Prodigal Son confronting Zeno's paradoxes

Ten years from today, in either direction, he is running toward himself. In both simultaneous instances, he carries an arrow. One version of him is building up speed to throw the arrow at some unsuspecting target, the other is being propelled by an arrow caught in midflight. To the one in the middle, the two runners appear as frozen images (or would appear as such if peripheral vision had no limits) and he feels himself expanding toward both of them, like a series of points along a line. To him, everything is in the plotting: there is no line without points, no surface without a line. Reason precedes existence. Why argue the matter? The line is not chalk on a sidewalk or a crack along the chalk mark; it is not the imprint of a fallen reed swallowed by wet sand—the explicitly sexual mouthful of water waiting to follow the sunken reed. Reason is the self-sufficient animal that devours itself in order to survive. The line is not a rope or a string or the section of barbed wire cut for the escape. He is running against the generally accepted notion that sees lines as the envoys of abstract distance. His dismantled agenda sets the pace.

# The Prodigal Son introduces George W. G. Ferris

to A. F. Möbius. Though both men are dead, he thinks enough has come full circle since 1893 for the meeting to take place without a hitch. Americans are as nervous about the world as they are about the missing years that must be found before the century can come to a happy conclusion, like a popular novel or a joke one pretends to be hearing for the first time. Strategically dangerous from any angle. It is so easy to jump in when a young comedian or a relative from the old country forgets the punch line or tells it incorrectly. Then there is this matter of latitude, how much one allows a joke to stray from the original, how easily adaptable or how awkward humor is when it leaves the culture that creates it. 1893: Chicago hosts the World's Columbian Exposition before another century loses its fight with the world. Ferris sees his wheel turn and he laughs as though this were a joke he has told himself many times, always pretending he has never heard it before. The wheel is all laughter, everyone on it privy to the same joke and easily distracted from the nature of the ride. Möbius cannot be outdone unless one is prepared to abandon laws of physics and some given of geometry. Only a great fire can twist the wheel, freeing it of its spokes. Only a great fire can keep the single surface of the twisted wheel rotating in place, circumference and center defined by the radius that burns between them.

## The Prodigal Son: Still life in slow motion

A blue decanter for the birds of paradise. He thinks they are actually birds and when the water evaporates he doesn't say the flowers have wilted; he tells you, instead, that the birds have died of thirst. This is as close as he comes to a vision of heaven though it's less than mythical, and fragile as a hollow bone. He hopes to find—days later, when he returns—the various components settled, like an argument. A blue decanter because the vase, Cézanne-green, is cracked; or because the stems of the flowers are too large and it will not occur to him, who thinks they are birds' legs, to trim them. Why not tulips, then? Or weeds, when a small assortment of these will do just as well? He tilts the empty decanter as if to pour, as if to demonstrate and witness the difference between pouring and spilling.

## *The Prodigal Son deconstructs the origami language*

that informs the syntax of his limbs. Beginning with the enormous, delicate wingspan—long, webbed digits fanning out majestically from his spine like a brittle cape. It is this version of himself that troubles him most deeply. It is this freedom that weighs him down, this hell-bent mythlike flightless self. Fortunately, this is his paper self, which folds like a row of lawn chairs at the end of summer, like summer itself under an onslaught of elms and sycamores. Each moment is carefully packed and put away and in each move at least one box is forgotten, but the future he leaves behind has nothing to do with the days that await him. The roads are lined with other creatures trying to sort themselves out—*endangered* on one side, *extinct* on the other; *distaff* on the left, *spindle* on the right. It makes the ride seem a little less hopeless. A tire blows out and the Falcon skids, stopping finally in the middle—exactly in the middle—of the road. He steps out to take a look at the flat, to see what he does not believe, and to discover in the process that there is symmetry even in an accident. He steps back, looks down and sees a nearly ordinary man looking up through the wing motif of the hubcap.

## The Prodigal Son, for whom summer is a verb

in the off-season, accidentally comes to grips with the largely incoherent letter of resignation signed by so many of his contemporaries. The names gather and sweep across the bottom of the page like a flock of small birds groomed by the thermal they ride. How can he question the signatures' authenticity when they are the only legible words in the letter? The birds are determined in their formation—a battalion charging with purpose; the impetus of a relentless world reaching into its own axis like Adam into the recesses of his imperfect rib cage, the maneuver performed for its own sake though from other worlds other Adams are most likely watching and taking notes and feeling for gaps between their own unfinished ribs which they read as their gods' ultimate disclaimer: perfection is attainable but unnecessary. There is often a single leaf—half green, half decomposed, and no sign of transition between one state and the other— left behind as proof or token. It is far more reliable than a feather, more likely to point to the arc of events, the sequence, whatever they call it nowadays, whatever leads birds out of their eggs and into the randomness that precedes the communal geometry of the flock, its skywriting abilities, the sky itself.

## The Prodigal Son pulls an all-nighter

*Do you wear a crumpled white suit? I do. Makes it easy to find myself in the dark.*

—Charles Simic

Even Purgatory has a waiting list. He has taken to wearing crushed velvet as a suitable euphemism. The dark, that ultimate texture for the palate, makes itself available as a violinist moonlighting for the hunger that still rises from the dance floor. In America they solve this problem with a fad known as the bottle club, which becomes a country called Enough when the parquet runs into the walls. Its citizens wait a lifetime to get all their papers in order, only to burn them, to declare themselves stateless in the hopes of being welcomed into the many arms of nothing. When they start to clamor for an instant folk hero, the fiddler finds himself in such demand that the bookings take up most of his time. What little he plays now is all pizzicato, nothing a banjo can't say just as well for a lot less.

2

## The Prodigal Son is caught off guard
## by planned obsolescence

A broom. The soles of his boots. The tires of his car, erasers, chalk, pencils, lead in the pencils. An ice sculpture. Stones in a river. Grain, millstone. Nothing strikes him until he comes across the man who sharpens blades for a living—scissors, axes, knives, cleavers. There's a perilous dance—a thing like courtship and sex and the wild disagreements of youth—between the blade and the whetstone: their reciprocal losses will amount to so little, or to so much, in the end. He walks on. A bar of soap. A rooster's beak, a hammer's claw. His own teeth. A pterodactyl. The steps between the square and the old cathedral. Inside the cathedral, a column pilgrims have been coming to touch for too many years. Very softly, with the tips of their fingers. The holes in the column show what centuries of tenderness will do. The fingernails of the living. Starlight. Sleep. Innocence. A hoe, a scythe, a pasture.

## The Prodigal Son, accompanied by the ideogram

for *instead*, attends the performance of a Cantonese opera. If there is no such symbol, he carves one in his arm. If the knife is blunt or the skin unyielding, he goes alone. If there is no opera, he sings to himself though the song of the goldfinch nesting in his one good lung is only a melodious cough. In the opera, a magician makes a fist and covers it with a scarf he has been waving very slowly. He lifts the scarf and produces a hypothesis. The vanished fist, still attached—hypothetically—to the magician's arm, will only return to the song of a goldfinch. The director insists on using a real bird. It dies just before making its entrance. The magician, oblivious to this, waves the scarf again. His disembodied fist materializes, clutching some feathers, in a birdcage carried by a peasant in another opera.

## The Prodigal Son as understudy

The pomegranate bites back. More than anthropomorphism, this is a ludicrous interpretation of what is commonly known as passive resistance. He lives in the attic and fasts before each performance though his part, for which he has yet to be called, is anything but crucial. He argues, nonetheless, that the play is driven by background tension and without so-called minor characters the whole thing might as well take place backstage. The pomegranate is invisible. It is difficult to tell our teachers from the agents of misinformation. This is Beethoven's "Fleur-de-lis," someone says, pulling the record carelessly from the sleeve and making a story to support the title, something about Ludwig and the French Foreign Legion. It is only by some slip of the tongue, years later, that he begins to say "Für Elise," and years after *that* realizes he has accidentally made a small correction with unfathomable repercussions. One must make adjustments. Leap years come to mind—every calendar at the mercy of February, the pendulums of Greenwich plotting a silent protest; one thinks of floodgates along the canal, their movements synchronized to keep the ocean on one side of the isthmus from spilling into the sea on the other side. He knows the drought and the law, keeps to himself during the state of emergency though he knows the bark of authority is only that; and there is little anyone can do to stop him should he decide to have company, cook indoors. They lift the ban as if it were a bandage and it rains pomegranates. He is secretly aware that the unfinished century is far from over.

## The Prodigal Son locates the epicenter

It's always better to forget. When the voice says *coordinates* he doesn't know if the news is about fashion or warfare, he's not even sure that it's news; it could be interference, unclaimed freight, the last word of an ecumenical hermit, a game of hopscotch without numbers, his hand, his other hand clutching dice in his pocket. There must be something palpable that separates *incidental* from *accidental*; otherwise, the suicide is mistakenly filed under *wrongful death* and life goes on as if this were the curtain, this the proscenium, this the cue to burst into the scene with an unintentional soliloquy.

*The Prodigal Son: Notes from the epicenter*

Moonglow, sunbeam, stardust. Light is the involuntary subtext when the topic is refraction. This is how rumors of a peripheral language get started. The edge recedes by increments so minuscule that we don't notice anything until a modest plot of land has grown like a spill of ashes. The wine list is often more engaging than the menu, like a woman who has learned to consolidate all the elements of her charm: once she greets us, everything else is nebulous. Like stardust. There are places where salvation speaks a language that consists of all the words we have refused. Moonglow. Sunbeam. Wet ashes, to be precise.

## The Prodigal Son paces the other half of a semicircle

He has been breathing mercenary weather. Much is discussed, plans and contracts are drawn up, marble slabs ordered from another continent. When the project is abandoned, only a spiral staircase has been erected. Something always intervenes. A centipede with multiple fractures drags the useless legs and makes its way along the banister, proving that there is no excess in the insect world. The absence of landscape is always demanding, like arpeggios when the fingers are cold and the joints swollen. It is not rising to the occasion that troubles him; it is the occasion itself, the irrefutable fact of it, how moments seldom conform to place. Dusk is heavy on his shoulders and he pauses to contemplate the burden.

*The Prodigal Son: Temporary trains*

Some transgressions are not forgivable. If that's not the case, our stay here is a horrible mistake. An inconsistency must've tipped them off at passport control—a tiny mole, a secret history of what they used to call incidents. The delegation arrives on schedule, but the interpreters have been delayed, reportedly detained for failing to carry their share of contraband. The word on the street is that they're being charged with numerous counts of attempting to obstruct a literal translation. A reasonable man may very well throw up his hands long before the skirmish escalates. The danger is that the hands often end up in the face of reason, right up against the eyes. One assumes. One starts to depend on assumptions. Here's the picture. This is how he looks when he's not looking.

*The Prodigal Son bribes the fortune teller*

"Dust off the superlatives and the leather vest. Prepare for another onslaught of arcane proportions. Here, get a handle on the new filing system before assuming your assigned position. The news leaks so rarely, and the little that seeps out is strictly second-rate material; what you get is a mirroring of the news, moisture building on the outside of a milk bottle. A reading of barometric pressure is always open to interpretation, like playing the 'Gentlewoman attending on Lady Macbeth' or conducting the premiere of an unfinished quartet with a series of optional bassoon interludes. They know you by your accounts of cultural trends—hush money, a flurry of distress signals—but they only remember your role in the highly acclaimed scandal. Proving that not all matter has substance is simple if you know your way back to the vacuum. Take a dowsing rod or a wishbone. You hear the sound of one shoe creaking as you walk; you stop and the sound continues. A sense-deprivation retreat will do you good. It's late Monday morning—the slate wiped bare with snake oil—before you know what hit you."

*The Prodigal Son: Standard deviations*

If what we miss is reflected in what we do, he must be walking those unmeasurable distances that keep us from going over the edge by keeping us from ever reaching the edge. The road is known to make allowances for its cargo—tilting a few degrees in one direction or another, the occasional decline or incline, the constant but imperceptible winding—and he takes advantage of the circumstances. Once the body learns to swerve or crouch to maintain its equidistance from the poison and the thorns of the foliage framing the path, the routine continues far into the season that tames the country. It's what he calls smooth sailing, especially now, on dry land, where the words mean more though they weigh significantly less. Turning a corner is the only difficult maneuver. The corner is always the edge (or part of the edge); conversely, there are edges without corners, infinite edges, stubborn ideas like roads that will not bend for a stand of birch trees.

## The Prodigal Son marks his calendar

for mid-December, maybe earlier, to give himself time to prepare,
time to go indoors and watch the year fall like a star into the sky of
another year. A simple exercise—in theory. Usually, however, things
are well on their way to an unwelcome randomness by June, the cal-
endar lost, the year already hopelessly small and slipping valuables
under its tongue. They find him leaning on the only signpost that
might guide him out of proportion to himself. He asks for one last
cigarette before morning. It's hard to get emotional about the facts.
He depends on faulty wiring and empty cupboards for his demon-
strations but often settles for the now incomplete set of dishes bought
long ago as an emergency gift, one of those things one stacks in the
closet just in case. This, he says, is what it's like to be impatient. It's
generally known, or assumed, he means disheartened. Dressing, he
skips a buttonhole on his shirt. This is not a code to be unfurled like
an awning. December is breath withheld; it is not, as one rumor
claims, a secret passed from the wrong hands to the wrong hands.
Spells of low pressure develop a disconcertingly objective pattern.
December is mirage weather, too many leaves in the house, a ser-
mon of consequences in place of the key under the doormat.

## The Prodigal Son swims to a barrier island

after the tsunami passes. FROM THE OUTSIDE LOOKING IN: everything is an island. Membranes fail. Chain-link fences. Cobwebs. Roads and bridges fail. His train of thought. A lucky streak. Another unexpected visitor fails to show up. FROM THE CENTER LOOKING OUT: even the untended sky is landlocked. Even a leaf floating on a pond. Even the water that keeps the pond from becoming nothing more than a crater again. FROM THE OUTSIDE LOOKING FURTHER OUT: the throat tightens a bit. FROM THE INSIDE LOOKING INWARD: a single eye covers the inconceivable dimensions of a point.

## The Prodigal Son learns to drown

Mannerisms have an inconsistent buoyancy and it's only a matter of time before they come up again, their gills sore, their sense of dislocation more acute. One arm rises as if filled with helium. A cheek twitches when the skin pulls itself inward. They're flooding the river for the first time in thirty years. To stir up sediments, to restore what some are calling a necessary disturbance. The head turns slightly to one side, then upward. When the jaw tightens, he almost gets that look he calls chiseled. The white torrent is very particular about what flows out at once, what remains untouched though not overlooked, what ricochets in the undertow. Engineers point out that water flowing at this rate can fill a skyscraper in seventeen minutes. The other arm, palm out, locks itself at an angle across his back. Engineers have more control over a single cell in the bloodstream than they have over how the canyon's face gleams in a certain light. Although they feel as familiar as his own hands, he recognizes none of the gestures. His heart takes longer pauses.

## The Prodigal Son envisions nothing

Eye behavior is, for the most part, learned behavior. He is taught to look others in the eye: his pupils make contact with other pupils like death rays in the old comic books. It isn't death that the act conveys, however; more than words or touch, it makes him sociable. Elsewhere he meets those for whom a look so direct and bold is threatening. So he teaches his eyes to close when he is having a conversation on a sidewalk or across a table. Once the mechanism is put in motion, his eyes close when he writes letters, they even close when he thinks of others. After some time, they forget to open at all, but memory, that third eye with no lid, repeatedly betrays his private darkness: every new town is impeccable until his imaginary eyesight stains the view.

## The Prodigal Son succumbs to secular miracles

This is the yard. (The fence, when he gets around to it, should begin and end in this corner.) Here's the shed and this is how he sees himself, at the appropriate moment, raking in the balance of an insufficient year. Neighbors are intimidated by the small posts marking the trajectory of the projected fence. A meeting is called. These are simple people, their collective fear their most compelling argument yet. There are several ways of looking at the absence of a fence though Stevens may not have the method nor Frost the mending tools. Perhaps if it were not a wall instead of not being a fence . . . A man and his neighbor are not one. The man, the neighbor and the fence they do not share add up to an inconclusive number. In its lifelong approach, the eye eventually focuses on the image, latches on to it, but it is the image that is blurred, a perfectly defined smudge to be interpreted as one interprets an apparition. Thirteen blackbirds descend with a single pair of wings on a tuft of flowers, a man sleeps off his belated absolution in a hammock between two unsuspecting trees.

## The Prodigal Son investigates the Hemingway suicides

And the list goes on. Like a parody ahead of its source. Sometimes the wreckage leaves no traces. A series of grinding halts picks up the trail where stepping stones have given in to too much walking. So the dots can still be connected, the distances covered without interruption. Sometimes the scrap pile is a small bruise; nevertheless, we insist on calling it an eyesore, calling it as if it could respond the way a dog responds to a note so high it crawls unnoticed into our ears like an intruder who ransacks the house while we sleep. We insist on calling it an eyesore as if it were something you could grind down just by rubbing it. Eyesore: not denoting something visually unappealing but calling attention to the pain of a strained cornea. Sometimes the clues are overwhelming, the narrative laid out like an abandoned city. This street this block this house this door this room this wall this nail half-driven into the wall as a preface to a photograph a watercolor a scapular that mistakes the nail for a neck this nail anticipating a hat a belt a memo a key ring a necktie whose width provides a context where the scene can be wedged. Sometimes dislocation is all it takes to anchor a hunch to a fact. He finds a voiceprint in his own ear and teaches it to speak. Leaning on the word *parapet,* he looks down the length of his vertigo.

## The Prodigal Son in absentia

In response to silence, more silence. An ordinary wind-driven device isolates his voiceprint without disturbing the rest of the Greek chorus. It is like wiping or peeling off the shadow cast by a passing object. The grand gestures are reenacted on his behalf but fail to arouse compassion. Trends may be the seams of history, but what guarantee do they offer? Mistranslations, typographical errors, and a symbol turns on itself like a bird flying repeatedly into a mirror: it can't tell one self from the other any more than we can tell a parasol—on a dry, overcast day—from an all-purpose umbrella. He knows what he sees, the rest he fills with language. Beauty is always incoherent; the fact that he can speak eloquently on the subject— the mere fact that he recognizes eloquence as an impostor would recognize his victim in a police lineup—is beginning to frighten him. He concludes that fear of beauty and fear of God are one. He waits for a self-propelled howl or moan, maybe the sound of things gathered inside a branch above one's head and gnawing at the wood when one is not paying attention. New recipes keep cropping up at traditional family meals until no one knows what is added and what, if anything, is authentic. If a deal is struck, he wants no part of it.

# 3

## THE PRODIGAL SON

## IN HIS OWN WORDS:

## Credo (1)

To find disharmony can be a blessing. Just imagine how foam left behind by a wave becomes a keepsake. A small tear in the fabric still has a certain charm when you look away instead of looking so perplexed. How foam left behind by a wave becomes a keepsake provided you have enough hands to hold it when you look away instead of looking so perplexed. At times it seems almost possible, this wish you're restoring, provided you have enough hands to hold it under a light so rigid it stings like a fish bone. At times it seems almost possible, this wish you're restoring. Something that real should not be seen; under a light so rigid, it stings like a fish bone. The day is safest where it intersects its deserters. Something that real should not be seen; just think of the pity you'll attract.

# Bees

There is a mathematical illusion that, if performed correctly, makes two halves mirror one another. We've seen enough disparities within the whole to know better. Some female bees mate only once. Carrying enough sperm for a lifetime, they continue to reproduce without further need for the male. Don't let the well-stocked shelves of the hardware store fool you: the part you need is never available. This is why the house deteriorates: hairline cracks appear, compromising the integrity of the structure, and your solution is another coat of paint. Door frames buckle and the doors never shut comfortably again. In one species of the mining bee, some females are never inseminated because their work is more valuable than any possible offspring. Pipes burst, filling the basement with water, and you can't find the right joint. I visit an excavation of my paternal ancestors' dwellings, built maybe three thousand years ago. Seen from higher ground, the community is an enormous honeycomb, the walls for the most part still standing solidly against the elements. My father's own house, by contrast, is barely habitable after only two centuries. Where I sleep, I do so with the uneasy feeling that I'll wake in a field, the house gone and the millennium gone with the house. Mason bees secrete their own cement. Though it may be rebuilt ad nauseam, the first house falls only once.

# Tipping over the actuarial tables

*No one in neuroscience thinks time is not important.*
*Criticisms arise with how time management is achieved.*
                    —Dr. Patricia Churchland, philosopher/brain scientist

1.

When handling the past in the present tense, chronology is of the utmost importance. Suppose I say *I'm eight years old and all the rooms of my father's house are larger than life.* Then I say *Two days after my first divorce, the only landscape I know is simplified, bone-smooth.* The past remains practically undisturbed. But suppose I reverse the order in which the episodes are recreated, and time goes on a rampage, and I find myself coming *and* going. Journeys on land have a spherical tendency because this is always at some level the nature of the terrain. The anthill crumbles in the rain and the ants returning with more provisions walk past the leveled mound; having noticed nothing, they keep looking for home. Though each mouth carries its crumb of sustenance, tradition and evolution will see to it that it isn't eaten until the journey has been completed. It's not unusual for the ants to walk repeatedly over the ruins. A squirrel chases itself so fast around the trunk of a palm tree that it appears to be standing still, like propeller blades in midflight. (I used to know the cause of this illusion.) I say *Someone's at the door, somebody please get the door* although I haven't lived there in years. *Somebody please get the door.* I want nothing more than my share of the past.

2.

True. There are degrees of isolation. Sixteen days after a shopping center collapses like a punctured lung in Seoul, South Korea, a nineteen-year-old girl is found alive in an elevator shaft. Her only nourishment throughout the ordeal is an apple that a monk gives her in a dream. The doctors are skeptical and attribute her survival, instead, to "her false perception of time." The brain—with its network of rivers and tributaries, the flow rigorously controlled—is taxed by a sudden drought. Or an apple passes from one hand to another. In both versions, extraordinary measures achieve a modicum of normalcy, shaken again when a boy—age thirteen, his circadian rhythms still fighting the syncopation of jet lag—walks out the window on the thirtieth floor of a Swedish building. They're calling it "a sleep-walking accident," as if sleep were a cognitive state. If that were the case, our sheep and our prayers would keep us up all night, counting and repenting, and there would be degrees of salvation. I can tell you that none of this is true, but much of it is, and you will not forgive me when you discover that I've led you to believe otherwise. The truth, in one form or another, has ways of finding you. Blame it on your false perception of the facts. Time the sniper has lapses in which its eyes tire and its focus falters and it aims at itself. So the window opens; the girl shakes the rubble from her dress; a monk, gathering apples in his robe, almost catches the falling boy.

3.

They say that when the Who performed at Leeds University on Valentine's Day 1970, Pete Townshend played against his own echo during some of those riveting excursions he launched into throughout the band's quarter-hour-long offering of "My Generation." I listen to it differently now. I wait for the echo they tell me is there, preceding each note, and it's as if I were experiencing the music a priori. I listen to chords or whole riffs bouncing off the walls versus sound in real time. Doing so, I miss the actual song, which is also delayed because this is, after all, a recording. Once, the concept of real time was redundant. Before the first gramophone. Before we learned to manipulate the speed of things to come. And long before that, the idea of a spirit that takes over for the temporary body was already popular. Perhaps our first attempt to deny the unavoidable. One new religion offers immortality. For a price. Unlike traditional religions in which death is a prerequisite, this one teaches the body to bypass the soul, that middle man who always gets in the way, and the here-and-now becomes a here-and-always. It's all up here, one of its members says to me, pointing his index finger at his temple, as if mimicking a gun. I may actually want to die before I get old, I think, the radio as loud as it'll go, one chord after another bouncing off the walls so many years ago at Leeds, the road much longer than I'd expected, the signal growing weaker and one station giving way to another. From feedback to static to a preacher who invites me or commands me or dares me to lay my hands on the radio. Both hands, he says. I raise my legs, raise my whole body (although it's not levitation or anything nearly as glamorous) to steady the steering wheel.

4.

In The Book of Ironies they forgot to write that a superstitious woman will end up marrying an atheist. Curiously, in all the cases I know, it's the man who doesn't believe. The woman is always open at the very least to the possibility of that "something out there." At times her superstitions are proof of God's constant tinkering with the cogs and wheels of the soul. There are atheists with proof of a finite world, atheists in need of a finite world, reformed atheists whose image of God has become so pure over the years that it has gone from inevitable to unnecessary to simply impossible. One believer argues that only the next life makes this one tolerable and lends it purpose, that only the idea of being part of something circular can keep us from going mad, because true madness is linear and the points at either end are clearly defined. This is an uncomfortable thought for her. I wonder if her belief is, more than anything, a way to keep at bay this linear derangement. The atheist lying beside her is beginning to sink into sleep when she speaks: she has carefully chosen this moment, thinking he's vulnerable enough to say what she wants to hear. He sits on the edge of the bed and wonders for a moment what it would be like to take that leap forward; or backward, which is something she doesn't mention: believers of her kind tend to discount any previous incarnations, as if eternity began here. Being here, he says to himself as he has said to her so many times, *is* the point. Then he tries to think his way back to sleep: wedding band, crown, zero, smoke ring, lasso, hula hoop.

## Homage to Li Po

From the water's uncertain edge I listen to the voices among the reeds. My own voice falls and rises in its alien tempo, and fails. The world doesn't last outside the spiral of days memorized by leaves turning. A sandpiper—before it can fly back, before it can think of home—has to struggle with the shore; home can always wait. Like the bird, I listen for the ebb tide: in the mounting silence, the flywheel that regulates our stay falls short of my expectations; camouflaged, it still leaves traces and doubts. Another day takes back its last hurrah and gives a second chance to the last light. (The extended hours begin to feel at home here; they mistake themselves for leaves about to be swept off; they listen for the next delayed morning—its footfalls, its signature song, the swirling layers of fly ash that belong nowhere else.) When the bird—flycatcher or sandpiper—at last outsmarts the tide and drinks, the act falls under some Darwinian category: home and distance as incentives: the bird listens more intently, its senses clear as flyleaves, every feather groomed. Ostensibly it leaves nothing to chance, but when attempting to fly again it forgets how to forget gravity, how to listen for the call from home, how to have the last word about reclaiming the nest. In exile, home is a story that breaks your fall from grace; you find yourself standing at the fall line, your back to the new plateau where leaves— your only possession—finally rest. When home is the name of every bird in sight, the need to fly supplants the need to see things last; you learn to sleep where nothing's grounded. Listen, listen: Fall's last leaves fly home.

*Rhetorical answers*

Under conditions that are only possible elsewhere, I tend to feel much better though I'm beginning to get the impression that things are improving locally. It hasn't been that long: I remember the road years, itineraries clouding my eyes. Time goes south when it's not in a hurry; it repeats itself in fragments. I'd have to be standing there, awake, to know how well or how miserably I sleep on any given night. Those few times I witness the dark dissolving into morning, the whole incredible thing is an afterthought revisiting itself. There is more to this than this, like the series of expectations in the case of the child who raises an arm, as if to pat herself on the head, and says, "I'm this tall," the hand still hovering inches above the uneven part in her hair. There is a partial end to everything. Each day, a different stranger passes for me; they differ from one another as much as I resemble every one of them.

## Credo (2)

The day is safest where it intersects its deserters. One always attempts to undo the scenery. Just think of the pity you'll attract if everything comes off exactly as you planned. One always attempts to undo the scenery while others are occupied with larger distractions. If everything comes off exactly as you planned, you will want to decipher that foreign tongue in your mouth while others are occupied with larger distractions at the foot of some decidedly obscene afternoon. You will want to decipher that foreign tongue in your mouth. It has been written and it has been erased at the foot of some decidedly obscene afternoon. Presumably, our civilization is content with an appetite for traffic: it has been written and it has been erased, but it sprouts again from the cracks in the road.

## Independence

Perhaps John Donne is on to something. A peninsula, convinced of its link to the continent, has insular delusions. One day it looks over its shoulder and sees an island, nothing more, and they are a single mass adrift and unnamed. The peninsula is unflinchingly stoic. It says nothing about other peninsulas that spring from the edges of continents. Its idea of adventure, when pressed to talk about such things, is taking a plunge to join a coral reef though one senses that, like most ideas, it will remain in its shrine—useful, reassuring, untouched. One pictures a fire alarm—or, in some of the older buildings, a hose—just beyond a fragile plate of glass that begs to be broken should the need arise. One can make a case for most things, especially when desire masquerades as need. The peninsula is by no means on a quest for isolation; it is, however, fiercely self-reliant— as long as the island doesn't loosen its grip.

*Captivity*


There is a moment of certitude followed by a life of overconfidence. This is neither the moment nor the life but the long stretch of teasers and fillers where one is inclined to follow the progress of certain novelty news items. "Zoo officials announce the birth of a two-headed snake." Strange what captivity does, how the body resumes what the imagination has abandoned, how the imagination grows slippery with use and even more slippery with disuse. A brief history of endings snuffs out the perpetual flame; you write a name in the smoke that follows. Some animals, though clever enough to design their own trap and scent it with magnetic north, don't have the patience to wait for the enemy who comes to chew off the leg caught in the clamp.

## Free will

The world keeps falling through the holes in my eyes. I'm amazed at the sky, at the way we have trusted the sky for so long, assuming it will keep coming back. On those days when my life seems a little too complete, I sit with the theologian from whom I've rented a room. To stir up conversation, one of us starts the usual litany: free will, God's will, responsibility, how Bach's cantatas seem inspired, how the Dodgers will have a better shot at the Series this year. My landlord likes to talk about the sun to make his point. Astronomers, he tells me, don't really have proof that the sun will rise again; they just have the odds on their side: the sun has been rising for as long as men have been keeping track, and why not assume it will rise again? That's not science; it's faith. And what about the Dodgers, I say. The Dodgers, he says, should take up astronomy.

*Fate*

Sir Isaac Newton has not considered the overripe asteroid, a prime factor (so one theory goes) in precipitating the extinction of the dinosaur. The likelihood of being hit by one of these dwarf planets today is as remote as the odds of ending up in the fist of a tornado. There ought to be some indemnity for phenomena of this magnitude. One could make a killing just amending life insurance policies in Kansas. Call it the Newton Clause, the Dorothy Principle, the dark variable in the plummeting $x$ or $y$. We leave apple season as we might leave a party we've crashed—with an exaggerated nonchalance that gives us away before we're out the door and headed for another overwhelming disappointment. A blunt and discriminating stillness in the wind prompts us to move to Kansas and up the ante. We demand to know if our contingency plans consider the possibility that the interstellar debris for which we're still preparing may have fallen while we were minding our earthly business.

# Faith

The unfamiliar must be followed if one is to go on; ideally, the responsibility of mapping the unknown falls on anyone but a cartographer. It's someone's job to expect us, someone's job to forget that we're on our way. We feel secure saying it; the words form and dissolve and form again and cling to the walls within us. It must be someone's job to clear the road for the ambulance, someone's job to sit in a particular chair so that it will never be empty; someone else's job to keep track of the chairs where no one, under any circumstances, must ever sit. I find a mound and feel secure in knowing, or believing, that it's someone's job to die, someone's job to bury, someone's job to stop the mound from becoming a hill in which the dead might feel neglected. We must be careful not to be misled: neglect is not alienation. Neglect—not the avoidance but the perpetuation of it—is also someone's job. The occasional stumbling of the otherwise graceful and the genuinely selfless albeit rare gestures of the cruel...Making sure each of these goes off with a hitch is certainly someone's job. It's someone's job to keep us on our toes, someone's job to keep us from knowing. Our job, if we have one of this nature, is likely to involve showing proof of where we are at any given moment. The penalty for disabling the tracking mechanism is life beyond one's means—and it looks like the damage is well underway.

## Credo (3)


Presumably, our civilization is content with an appetite for traffic. What was once acceptable eventually gets outlawed, but it sprouts again from the cracks in the road, as when a handful of gestures replaces a cantata. What was once acceptable eventually gets outlawed. Everything fits in your pocket or remains unfinished, as when a handful of gestures replaces a cantata and the night watch is extended indefinitely. Everything fits in your pocket or remains unfinished—the etiquette of feudalism, mantelpieces, clocks that need oiling—and the night watch is extended indefinitely. This is our best view yet of the old countries, the etiquette of feudalism, mantelpieces, clocks that need oiling for an allegory of insurmountable sadness and thirst. This is our best view yet of the old countries' legacies: reversible uniforms, flags turned to soil.

## Benedictus

Bless the shotgun shack but not the buckshot that names it    Bless the hands that aim the barrel at the open door    Bless the space between the door and the window    Bless the window already shattered when the shot flies out    Bless the shattered glass that is someone's bed    Bless the heavy sleep of a short night but not the sleeper the pain but not the wound the concept of thirst and the idea of a throat but not thirst itself or the throat where thirst settles like a palpable word    Bless language but not speech    Bless the invention of the aqueduct and all the missing links that follow an invention until it's either obsolete or forgotten    Bless the years of reconstruction the rains and floods and droughts and useless crops the next reconstruction and the next one and the one that falls on itself not because it can't help its own demise but because it *can*    Bless the brief itineraries the temporary schedules the time lines on the wall the time lines on the surface of the river    Bless the creek but not the bridge    Bless the pot on the stove and the water in the pot and the fire but not the fuel that makes the fire that boils the water    Bless the straw roof and her kin the straw man who stands guard beyond the window    Bless the nothing-here-to-steal look on the straw man and the vastness that supports his look like a blessing    Bless the man and the look but not the eyes    Bless the mud floor but not the mud    Bless one wall bless only one wall and maybe the open door    Bless the god-awful the god-heavy the godforsaken    Bless the sin of wishing for another window

## Prayer against Ecclesiastes

Budding leaves on a dying tree. *Alpha* like a grain on the tongue.
The first and only word. A sigh. Under this sun each thing is new
and incomplete. Water from melting snow doesn't flow out of sight
in shame. Another school of salmon answers the gravitational pull
of a heavy sky. Even our losses are fresh: in its finite wisdom each
thing—virginity, a good crop—leaves a taste of itself: the last and
only absence, and *alpha* like nothing on the tongue again.

*Letter to the anarchists*

For a long time, the concertmaster is in charge of the orchestra as well as his own instrument. It is his job to keep time, the bow a metronome, his arms almost mechanical in their transition from one role to the other. He approaches the task leisurely, seeing the ensemble as an appendage of the violin. By the time he concludes, it is as though the violin were the last instrument on the planet and this monumental sound its voice. Once a conductor is introduced, the concertmaster becomes, how shall we say, second fiddle. There are plans for a mutiny, but the percussionists are always too far back to hear and the music goes on. The conductor, like a drug feeling more at home in the bloodstream, commands a little less authority each time he stops a rehearsal and singles out one musician who is slightly off. The musician frequently challenges the conductor—a momentary snag in an episode bound to run its course, like a woman stopping to check her lipstick on her way to an appointment for which she is already late. Though we want to keep time without him again, the conductor somehow seems as necessary as time itself. His arms go limp and we carry him to the podium, prop him up, imagine him guiding us. Our music, meanwhile, grows shamelessly atonal. Impressionism sees to it that we get through that, easing whatever pain the loss of color causes. Music grows muddy—the result of too much color—and we scrub the notes clean, one by one; we bleach polyphony out of the fabric, blaming texture for the decline, but music grows louder. Music grows anxious. Music interferes with the din of the world. Music defies the composer. The conductor defies the composition and collapses. The concertmaster calls for a permanent return to the sensible design of dissonance.

*Debussy*

"Grownups," writes Claude Debussy in 1901, "tend to forget that as children they were forbidden to open the insides of their dolls." This, he claims, is why they end up "poking their aesthetic noses into things that don't concern them." Marco Polo and Neil Armstrong are only looking for a new clock whose gears they can inspect. We go out of our way to hear the ticking of a bad heart or the ticking of the stars. Our towns are built on piles of broken dolls. There are cracked porcelain cheeks at the bottom of the sea, torn stuffed limbs in deep space. We're all guilty of what Debussy calls "a crime of high treason against the cause of mystery."

## Credo (4)

For an allegory of insurmountable sadness and thirst, the far sky drops apologetically out of sight. Legacies, reversible uniforms, flags turned to soil—sometimes a shadow lands on an image and doesn't regain its strength. The far sky drops apologetically out of sight. It's late. We've been standing for a long time at the end of a continued fraction. Sometimes a shadow lands on an image and doesn't regain its strength if the story holds. I'd like to tell it again: It's late; we've been standing for a long time at the end of a continued fraction, one hand on the law of best intentions, the other on its promise to bring us back. If the story holds, I'd like to tell it again. Maybe the breeze lifts her skirt and you sigh, one hand on the law of best intentions, the other on its promise to bring us back. A small tear in the fabric still has a certain charm. (Maybe the breeze lifts her skirt and you sigh.) To find disharmony can be a blessing. Just imagine:

4

## The Prodigal Son's education

How the horizon knows that we're coming    Why the horizon is always a step or two or a lifetime ahead of us    How coincidence intrudes in our plans    How we said we'd end up    What we've become    Where we are    Why eternity comes to terms with its makers    How our handful of time is beginning to look somewhat small for the task we've been assigned    The task    How we go about it    Why time is a single hand doing the work of two

## The Prodigal Son forgives his brother

When summer gets too loud, they collect crickets. They put them in a box and give them leaves to eat. And poke holes in the box—not to let them breathe, as one might reasonably assume, but to be able to see what goes on inside. In one of those rare moments when bewilderment binds the two boys, they peek through holes at opposite ends of the box and wink at each other. Between them, two crickets are mating or struggling to flee; it's difficult, especially when one is so young, to recognize and name the various desires. They see the crickets eat too much and they will see them starve. A curious sound seeps out of the box, a muted echo that varies depending on where the crickets are in relation to any hole or combination of holes. Just think of how fingers work on a wind instrument. The older boy studies the pattern of the crickets' conversation and begins to imitate one of the voices. He wants to understand it, but has to settle for this ability to speak Cricket the way some singers learn to sing in a foreign language: phonetically and with complete ignorance.

## The Prodigal Son on a bus in New Delhi

Every word eventually becomes corrupt. When someone greets him, the voice decidedly foreign but familiar, he discovers that his name is a Hindustani insult. There ought to be a warning, a periodic table of language, a grid on which all the known words are arranged by their atomic weight. The word that is his name fills the crowded bus with the odorless resoluteness of a paralyzing agent designed for a war that was never fought. The other passengers look at him as they would look at the mother of a crying child. Like the mother who apologizes for her child's behavior, he feels responsible for the weight of his name, for its reliable atomic structure and its ability to taint the status quo like a revolutionary in flames. He adopts his brother's name for the remainder of his indefinite stay.

## The Prodigal Son buries a dog named Pavlov

In a land where men greet each other with a kiss on each cheek, he remembers his father. The objectivity of metaphors assaults him and he wants to accept it, believe in it, handle it like a container that has taken on the shape of the liquid it once carried, but he doesn't make a move before drawing a clear line between the artificial pairings of fiction and those natural links from the reassuring small talk of his rural encounters. He doesn't think of his father, which is something one does willingly; he remembers. And this is what he remembers: *The father is inside the door; the son is already standing outside, leaning in, so most of him is still in the house.* When he meets a man now, he pulls back, pulls away like an injured animal that has finally learned the meaning of each approaching scent. He remembers the gentle pacing of his father going in and out of rooms, mixing anecdotes with warnings about a world in the wings, something severe always at the root of his voice. He sees himself retreating as his father kisses him. He feels the sting of the old man's benediction, the two-day beard, the dust that gathers in his pores. A farewell is merely an unfinished greeting finally put to rest. The improbable syntax of that time decomposes as it calls: all he hears now is the idea of home.

## The Prodigal Son takes up a hobby

*The face was no more capable of expression than a block of gnarled wood.* —Sir Frederick Treves, on John Merrick (the Elephant Man)

Woodcarving, if you don't mind. It's a way of passing the time, a way to carve a path he cannot travel. He carves a flower and he carves a spear and he sees how the two are one and the same. Then he sees nothing and says to himself that the wood is damaged, very possibly sabotaged. He makes a door and forgets the hinges. He makes cabinets and wooden sandals and a bread box. He used to keep fresh eucalyptus branches in the house because the leaves, while they were green, made him feel as though he wasn't home. Now he carves a leaf into what used to be the trunk of a eucalyptus tree. It's a primitive leaf, a minimalist leaf, barely an outline: he lets the meticulously layered imperfections of the wood take over: rings and knots form the veins of the leaf.

## The Prodigal Son: Studies for a portrait of John Merrick

The true affliction of the Elephant Man is his left arm, which has developed, according to Sir Frederick Treves, into "a delicately shaped limb covered with fine skin." In the context of any other body, the arm might've gone unnoticed, its beauty reduced to a fraction of the more imposing beauty that is the world in which a body moves. He wants to capture something crucial about Merrick, whose last days are spent building a cardboard model of a cathedral. Merrick's head is so heavy with longing that he has to sleep with his body propped up by pillows. He starts by drawing Merrick lying down, stretched out and sleeping very peacefully: it defies reality so boldly. And that's why it won't do. So he draws Merrick sitting down, his eyes closed. This won't do either. He draws the geometrically impossible shape of the head, the unimaginable face, the nose "only recognizable as a nose from its position." (Without a reference point, what would Sir Frederick have called the shape?) Because this one won't do, he draws Merrick, his back to us, looking out the window: the sources of his miniature—two churches, one of them still under construction—rise among the buildings of London like lost tourists scanning the panorama, taking in all the foreign air their lungs can hold. The only finished drawing is the one of Merrick's "beautiful hand which any woman might have envied," its fingers shaping a spire for the tiny cathedral of longing that rests like an exhausted head on the table.

## The Prodigal Son is spotted on the grassy knoll

—again. The question would be moot but for the fact that a single bullet has generated so many overlapping and contradictory theories; it would have all been over long ago if we had not kept asking ourselves what are the facts in the fact. The crowd—the cold-blooded, stain-resistant crowd—is his weapon of choice. He is whistling "The Yellow Rose of Texas" to himself, but the song crashes into the slanting wind. This is found music at its corrosive best. John Cage might have called it accidental but necessary music; he might have said no composition is subject to the same interpretation twice, implying that written music is mostly not written and certainly never finished. Cage notwithstanding, his motive is yellow roses, tiger lilies in a tin can; it is the whistling itself.

*The Prodigal Son, briefly suspected in the shooting*
*of Andy Warhol, is cleared of all charges*

One day in late summer 1982, twenty years after the flower shop first delivered them, they will stop coming, but in 1968 Joe DiMaggio still has half a dozen long-stemmed roses placed by Marilyn's crypt every Tuesday, Thursday and Saturday. By Monday, June 3rd, the fresh-cut bunch left over the weekend has done its job. The year will be remembered for the scent of flowers and gunpowder and a song with a passing reference to Joltin' Joe. We're desperate and desperation makes us larger than life in each other's eyes though life itself is not as large as we picture it. By this time next year some of us will be packing for the moon, the rest of us will be driving out to the country, and only the wounded will remember where they were today.

## The Prodigal Son stands outside the Dakota

playing night watchman or some other profession on the verge of
invisibility. He plays doorman, bows, tips his imaginary cap. He
plays elevator man. One day the king is polishing the stones on his
crown when the Constitution strikes him on the head like lightning.
A warning shot. (The lengths to which a country will go to keep its
patron saint from decomposing!) The ambassador makes life miser-
able for his chief of protocol, who finally resigns. And grins as he
leaves the ambassador to deal with a wet cigar unraveling like a myth
of swallows above the sacred ruins whose very destiny is being nego-
tiated. Diplomacy can be brutal. The night of the cease-fire there is
ice on the roads, but the more daring skaters have headed south in
search of an apolitical climate. (If they only knew how fiercely par-
tisan the weather can be.) Let the record show the weight of the
crime: a voice shouts fire in an empty auditorium and the crowds
rush in.

## The Prodigal Son as decoy

To tap (into) the absolute music of the bones; irrepressible, nearly scandalous womb-sap where one story folds and unfolds repeatedly. *When in a big city, never look up. Even if skyscrapers beckon like seductive whispers, keep your eyes on the city-within-the-city that exists only at eye level—that traffic light still a block away; the pedestrians who ignore it and cross, weaving leisurely among stalled vehicles. Be vigilant, but look distracted by the mundane components of the day: avoid shop windows, resist the lure of their seasonal tableaux.* Temptation is listening, it has been listening for a long time; now it stands here and there, waiting for eyes that seem to wander away from that bouquet of chaos whose blossoming gives a city its pace. Smooth Temptation works the streets dressed as the quintessential newcomer, asking where's the station when does the last one leave the city what time is it how do I get this package overseas. It is a creature of daylight. In quiet, isolated towns it still does the movies early, goes from one feature to the next with a single stub. By the time the usher aims his flashlight as if holding all the power of the galaxy at the root of that beam, Temptation has subsided and reemerged elsewhere. The usher runs to the lobby, where he notices for the first time how the girl in the booth under the marquee tears all-purpose tickets from a roll.

## The Prodigal Son: Science fiction

On the heavy surface of another planet he approaches her casually, like a man walking off a meal, though the man he has become is propelled by an ever-increasing hunger, the meal always ahead, the planet always on the verge of some catastrophic event. Each night they go out to count the moons—an old habit—but lately he's had trouble finding them all. When he turns to ask her *How many do you see now?* he senses their two bodies occupying the same space. One body doubles its mass and the other becomes nothing but breath. The shared responsibility is horrifying: if he's the flesh, he must remember and avoid everything that takes her breath away; if, on the other hand, he's the breath, he can't afford to get lost in the body, or on his way back to it, as he so often does.

## The Prodigal Son in spite of himself

This is the only (au/oral) record of it—the inflections, the wow and flutter of the subject. He says *The light is abundant.* She says *Bountiful.* (There are such subtleties in the light! so many gradations!) He says *Light as an ax*, treating *light* as a noun; then he says *Light rain* to describe the sign flickering in a downpour outside their window. She says *Incandescence* because it seems like a safe, frugal way of summing up a state of rapture. This here—everything you don't see, everything you couldn't possibly imagine—is the mouth, the disembodied mouth that speaks for both of them, the thing before and the thing instead of, a succession of Russian dolls—egg-shaped, hollow, halved—giving up smaller versions of themselves, like words shedding syllables. They line up—the words, the dolls—in descending order, their bodies now more than ever in need of continuity.

## The Prodigal Son loses his wife

It's not what you think. They are walking in a crowd when she suddenly dissolves. Tired of looking, he tells himself she must have gone home. At home, he finds the children waiting, demanding to know where their mother is. Understandable, he thinks, but he's sure she's on her way back. It was a small crowd, after all, and she couldn't possibly have gone too far. But the children soon grow restless. There have been numerous reports lately of missing people suddenly showing up in a strange family. The children want to know if their mother is watering blue geraniums on someone else's terrace. They propose an all-out search, but the father becomes suspicious, believes that they want to plant in him whatever seeds of guilt they've managed to find around the house. He thinks they've been through his papers, in his pockets, and under his mattress. One day he cannot remember his wife. He sees the children and tries to find her face in theirs, but it does not come. He listens for her voice in the voices of the children and only hears the children.

## The Prodigal Son buys a new car

because he has outgrown the one he bought when he outgrew the motorcycle they gave him when he outgrew his feet. In the interim he has outgrown all his clothes, houses, marriages, his two children, and the one language he thought he had mastered. Briefly he works as a banker, but decides to quit when he notices that he is becoming too attached to the concept of saving. Now he refers to it as his "nice little job in the warehouse." In a recurring dream he's been having lately, he's wearing a suit and operating a forklift, moving pallets of money from one end of a warehouse to the other and back. Brand-new bills, large bills, all neatly wrapped and stacked. Beats driving a brand-new car, he says.

## The Prodigal Son: Vegas, after hours

Walking toward a phone booth, he tucks in the wrinkled shirt, because these things matter, and wonders what it would be like to stand in the halo of a nuclear blast. He wants to be a raving lunatic, talk to himself as loudly as those people who walk around talking back to God, but suspects that the line of communication with the self is damaged or busy this morning. Perhaps he's already getting through and doesn't know it. (In a time he wants to call better, his children make telephones out of tin cans linked by a string. When the older one gets tired of pretending, the younger child runs from one can to the other, saying *I'm gonna catch myself.* Meaning, one assumes, the voice.) There's a woman in the phone booth. Because she's not talking, he can't tell if she's listening intently to someone or getting up the courage to dial. Or to hang up. He's fascinated by his own patience, maybe alarmed. He thinks of traffic, his last conversation and engines running on diesel fuel at the other end of the line, how one distinctive sound marks an ordinary place.

# The Prodigal Son and the epistemology of chance

*Further evidence shows that we have reached the point of maximum risk.* —Alan Greenspan, Chairman, U.S. Federal Reserve

Just outside of Reno, Nevada, he realizes that he left his wallet on the nightstand. He thinks of the argument at the motel and wonders if the maid he insulted has picked him clean. Looking for a good place to make a U-turn, he reviews a mental inventory of all the amulets in the wallet—a strip of pop wisdom from a fortune cookie *(People who don't know where they're going usually wind up somewhere else)*, the only photograph he owns in which everyone is more than likely still alive, the horoscope that says *You will travel,* and a crude map with a phone number and no name. He's almost certain it's a map to the house of someone who said *Write down my number in case you get lost.* All this time he has entertained the thought of calling to say *I'm always here,* but it would sound too melodramatic even in jest. He passes a break in the median and keeps going. At every good opportunity to turn back, he decides to go on. He drives into Reno in time for breakfast.

## The Prodigal Son in Pompeii

He covers his face with the palms of his hands, as if to read in broken Braille what he cannot feel; he wants to make more palpable the turbulence in his eyes and in his mouth—all those things they say about him, all that anguish—but all he gets from this is a permanent impression, on his hands, of his rather ordinary features.

## The Prodigal Son: Amnesty

In one of the photographs from Giza, he's riding the obligatory camel whose humps, through the generosity of perspective, appear as tall as the pyramids that rise in the background. So much is missing. In those reckless early days just after the West discovers the region, eternity is disturbed by thieves. He wonders, in the letter that accompanies the snapshots, what has happened to the loot over the years. He writes about the Nile, about the time he came so close to blowing up the Aswân High Dam, how sometimes he regrets the attempt and sometimes he regrets having walked away. He says that you can actually see the shape of history being defined and deformed by the river and its floods. There are ruins more beautiful in their decay than most human faces in their prime. Ultimate justice, he says, must be something like Olympus or Valhalla (as far as he knows, Egyptians have yet to name the place) turned inside out at the other end of the eternal spectrum, an empty field where every dead pirate, every vandal of mummies and canopic jars, returns something stolen, and the pile grows into a spontaneous monument to us and to itself.

## The Prodigal Son accidentally kneels
## while learning to crawl

It is difficult to say whether the church was named for a saint or for someone named after a saint. It is a small church. Around him and seemingly closing in, the pained faces of those intermediaries. The flaking paint reveals a heightened sense of agony in their expressions. When you get to a certain level, they all share a single expression. It is not sacred, but it might as well be, coming from the anonymous hands that molded these bodies and gave them their first coat of paint. He thinks of the statues baking like corpses. One wall is filled with plaques: he reads the names of the various families—these seekers of immortality—that have remodeled the church over the years. He wonders what happens when even the names are no longer here, what happens to the pain when the scaffold outlives the last patron of hope. In the cold and humid half-light, each saint, even after all the faces are stripped to the first expression, seems to have a particular pain. He remembers that look on himself: he wakes in a strange house and splashes water on his face, which rises slowly to meet itself at the mirror. It is late and the lights are out. The only face he can construct is one of a damaged saint suddenly aware of the difficulty in distinguishing between spiritual and sexual ecstasy; how the proper attire for both occasions is a burning robe; how the body goes through the same transformations before one altar as it does before the other; how muscles and tendons react to the touch of one god just as they react to the touch of the other; how the condition, regardless of how it manifests itself, is a desire for immortality, which is always profane.

## The Prodigal Son considers a diplomatic career

Out of respect for the elders of the village where he finds himself sober for the first time in years, he shows reverence for their gods and doesn't laugh at their icons. They believe him and make him a holy man. Fearing that the villagers might be contagious, and thinking only of himself, he seals their wounds and concocts potions for their pains. They trust him and make him a healer. To show his vulnerability, he bathes in a small pond with the men, eats from their unwashed plates, sleeps with their women. As they parade by his bed, the villagers dry the cold sweat from his forehead and call him a martyr. He tells them that his condition is temporary. When he regains his strength and gets up, they call him a prophet. He predicts that from time to time, in their sleep, the women will hear the voices of the gods. The elders tell him that the women have always heard the voices of the gods. They call him a fraud and make him chief.

## The Prodigal Son learns the word "antebellum"

after the peace accord is signed. It is much like the delayed reaction of one who is attacked by a mad archer and later describes it in terms of weight instead of pain, in terms of how the thing pulls him under, so to speak, instead of how one arrow rips through his leg or how the next one nearly misses his heart. The first sensation is never the truth. This is the small but crucial difference between Cupid and Romeo though they both stand beneath the balcony, defying its impending collapse. They feel safe in the shared and unfounded belief that the cracks bypass the balcony, affecting only its metaphors. The war creates its own inverted metalanguage, a sweet camouflage of the tongue. When the orders are issued and carried out, historians are recording the sound of helicopters caged between the napalm parentheses that prevent questions from getting off their knees to mingle with statements and raise questions of their own.

## The Prodigal Son overhears his interrogators

"Show him the left shoulder of the woman whose body tastes like rain; show him her shoulder and ask him to name the woman." "Show him his brother's fist and his father's fist; ask him why one thumb is wrapped by the fingers and the other thumb is exposed and clearly making the fist; ask him which one is heavy with anger, which one is aching. Show him veins bulging on the backs of his mother's hands and ask him something about the heart." "Ask him to identify his children from strands of hair." "Show him the eyes of an enemy." "Better yet, show him the space between the eyes. Show him the soles of his own feet; ask him if he thinks he can outrun them."

# CODA

## The Prodigal Son catches up with the bounty hunters

There is only one answer and even the bread crumbs stand at attention when it comes. Someone starts to talk about alleged disappearances, but is soon interrupted and the subject is closed. They bring him up to date on all the deaths in the family, the marriages, the births. In the wake of the latest scandal, they tell him, the new government has maintained its innocence, blaming the Constitution, blaming the scholars and "their gross misinterpretation of our laws." Tap water is potable for the first time in years. The house fell and was rebuilt at least three times, always on a different site. There was a war, they admit, although that's not what they want to say. There was famine. Their lungs and then their chests and finally their mouths fill with all the things they'd like to tell him. He knows the answer, but likes to hear them say it. After hovering, after spying like an insect on the screen door, he asks if perhaps there's a place for him at the table.

# NOTES & DEDICATIONS

The Marcus Aurelius quote is from his *Meditations* (Maxwell Staniforth, tr.; Penguin Books, 1964).

Count Basie's ad-lib is heard between false endings of his orchestra's 26 July 1955 recording of "April in Paris."

"The Prodigal Son and the two Sinatras" is for Luis and Mary Elizabeth Pérez.

"The Prodigal Son reassesses Kierkegaard": Che Guevara's inspirational words ("Hatred as a fighting factor, uncompromising hatred toward the enemy which pushes a human being beyond his natural limitations and transforms him into an effective, selective and cold killing machine. That is how our soldiers must be, a people without hatred cannot triumph over a brutal enemy.") were printed on what was quite literally a license to kill, awarded to a Cuban soldier who'd met the requirements to join the "special troops"; dated 8 March 1986, the certificate was found in the soldier's pocket two years later in Angola. (To be faithful to the original, I kept its awkward punctuation.)

"The Prodigal Son: Still life in slow motion" is for Cecilia Denegri.

"The Prodigal Son paraphrases a plagiarist": The Dalí-Millet link is explored in Salvador Dalí's "paranoiac-critical interpretation," *The Tragic Myth of*

*Millet's Angelus* (tr. from the French by Eleanor R. Morse; The Salvador Dalí Museum, 1986).

"Credo (1–4)" can be read as a single, uninterrupted poem.

"Homage to Li Po": I borrowed the idea of a prose sestina from Mark Strand.

"Free will" is for Mary Katherine Wainwright.

"Fate" is for Don Cason.

"Benedictus" (sans bullets) is for Kyle Pennington.

"Debussy" is for Peter Meinke. Quoted material, originally published in the 1 April 1901 issue of *La revue blanche*, appears in *Debussy on Music* (collected and introduced by François Lesure; Richard Langham Smith, tr. and ed.; Cornell University Press, 1988).

"The Prodigal Son on a bus in New Delhi" is for Dexter Filkins.

The epigraph of "The Prodigal Son takes up a hobby" and fragments quoted throughout "The Prodigal Son: Studies for a portrait of John Merrick" are taken from an excerpt of Sir Frederick Treves's *The Elephant Man and Other Reminiscences* (Cassell & Co., Ltd.) reprinted in Ashley Montagu's *The Elephant Man: A Study in Human Dignity* (E. P. Dutton, 1979).

# ABOUT THE AUTHOR

Dionisio D. Martínez, born in Cuba in 1956, is the author of *Bad Alchemy* (1995), *History as a Second Language* (1993), and *Dancing at the Chelsea* (1992). He has received fellowships from the Guggenheim Foundation, the National Endowment for the Arts, and the Whiting Foundation. His poetry has been published in numerous journals and anthologies, including *The New Republic, The American Poetry Review, Seneca Review, Colorado Review, Denver Quarterly, The Norton Anthology of Poetry* (1996), *The Best American Poetry* (1992 & 1994), and *Hard Choices: An* Iowa Review *Reader* (1996). His essays and reviews appear in the *Atlanta Journal-Constitution,* the *Miami Herald,* and the *St. Petersburg Times.* He lives in Tampa, Florida.